What This Guide Will Do For You

Whether travelling to a foreign country or to your favorite international restaurant, this *Nice & Easy* guide gives you just enough of the language to get around and be understood. Much of the material in this book was developed for government personnel who are often assigned to a foreign country on a moment's notice and need a quick introduction to the language.

In this handy and compact guide, you will find useful words and phrases, popular expressions, common greetings, and the words for numbers, money, and time. Every word or phrase is accompanied with the correct pronunciation and spelling. There is a vocabulary list for finding words quickly.

Generous margins on the pages allow you to make notes and remarks that you may find helpful.

If you expect to travel to Romania, the section on the country's history and relevant up-to-date facts will make your trip more informative and enjoyable. By keeping this guide with you, you'll be well prepared to understand as well as converse in Romanian.

Carl Fuchs
Language Program Director

Contents

ROMANIAN
Made Nice & Easy!™

Staff of Research & Education Association
Carl Fuchs, Language Program Director

Based on Language Courses developed by the
U.S. Government for Foreign Service Personnel

Research & Education Association
61 Ethel Road West
Piscataway, New Jersey 08854

Dr. M. Fogiel, Director

ROMANIAN MADE NICE & EASY™

Printed in the United States of America

Library of Congress Control Number 2001087401

International Standard Book Number 0-87891-401-3

LANGUAGES MADE NICE & EASY is a trademark of Research & Education Association, Piscataway, New Jersey 08854

ROMANIA

FACTS & HISTORY

Official Name: Romania

Geography
Area: 237,499 sq. km. (91,699 sq. mi.); somewhat smaller than New York and Pennsylvania combined.
Cities: *Capital*–Bucharest (pop. 2.02 million). *Other cities*–Constanta (344,000), Iasi (350,000), Timisoara (327,000), Cluj-Napoca (334,000), Galati (331,000), Brasov (316,000).
Terrain: Consists mainly of rolling, fertile plains; hilly in the eastern regions of the middle Danube basin; and major mountain ranges running north and west in the center of the country, which collectively are known as the Carpathians.
Climate: Moderate.

People
Nationality: *Noun and adjective*–Romanian(s).
Population: 22.5 million (est.).
Annual population growth rate:–2.7%
Ethnic groups: Romanians 89%, Hungarians 7.1%, Germans 0.5%, Ukrainians, Serbs, Croats, Russians,

Turks, and Gypsies 2.5%.
Religions: Orthodox 86.8%, Roman Catholic 5%, Reformed Protestant, Baptist, and Pentecostal 5%, Greek Catholic (Uniate) 1%, Jewish less than 0.1%.
Languages: Romanian (official). *Other languages–* Hungarian, German.
Education: *Years compulsory–*10. *Attendance–*98%. *Literacy–*98%.
Health: *Infant mortality rate* (1998 est.)–22/1,000. *Life expectancy–*men 69.5 yrs., women 73.9 yrs.
Work force (9 million): *Agriculture–*42.3%. *Industry and commerce—*38%. *Other–*34%.

Government
Type: Republic.
Constitution: November 21, 1991.
Branches: *Executive–*president (head of state), prime minister (head of government), Council of Ministers. *Legislative—*bicameral Parliament. *Judicial–*Constitutional Court, Supreme Court, and lower courts.
Subdivisions: 40 counties plus the city of Bucharest.

Economy
GDP: $38.2 billion.
Annual GDP growth rate: 4.5%.
Per Capita GDP: $1,328.
Natural resources: Oil, timber, natural gas, coal, salt, iron ore.
Agriculture (1998): 16.4% of GDP. *Products–*corn,

wheat, potatoes, oilseeds, vegetables, livestock.
Industry: 40.1%: *Types*–machine building, mining,
construction materials, metal production and processing, chemicals, food processing, textiles, cloth-
ing.
Services: 43.4%.
Trade: *Exports*–$8.3 billion: textiles, chemicals, light
manufactures, wood products, fuels, processed met-
als. *Major markets*–Germany, Italy, France, and
Turkey. *Imports*–$11.8 billion: fuel, cooking coal,
iron ore, machinery, wheat, cotton, and potatoes.
Major suppliers–Italy, Germany, Russia, France, and
U.K.

Geography

Extending inland halfway across the Balkan Pen-
insula and covering a large elliptical area of 237,499
square kilometers (91,699 sq. mi.), Romania occu-
pies the greater part of the lower basin of the Danube
River system and the hilly eastern regions of the
middle Danube basin. It lies on either side of the
mountain systems collectively known as the
Carpathians, which form the natural barrier between
the two Danube basins. Romania's location gives it a
continental climate, particularly in the Old Kingdom
(east of the Carpathians and south of the Transylvanian
Alps) and to a lesser extent in Transylvania, where the
climate is more moderate. A long and at times severe
winter (December-March), a hot summer (April-July),

and a prolonged autumn (August-November) are the principal seasons, with a rapid transition from spring to summer. In Bucharest, the daily minimum temperature in January averages 7°C (20°F), and the daily maximum temperature in July averages 29°C (85°F).

People & Culture

About 89% of the people are ethnic Romanians, a group that — in contrast to its Slav or Hungarian neighbors — traces itself to Latin-speaking Romans, who in the second and third centuries A.D. conquered and settled among the ancient Dacians, a Thracian people. As a result, the Romanian language, although containing elements of Slavic, Turkish, and other languages, is a romance language related to French and Italian. Primarily a rural, agricultural population, the medieval Wallachians and Moldavians maintained their language and culture despite centuries of rule by foreign princes. Once independent, the population of the unified Romanian state took their modern name to emphasize their connection with the ancient Romans.

Hungarians and Gypsies are the principal minorities, with a declining German population and smaller numbers of Serbs, Croats, Ukrainians, Greeks, Turks, Armenians, Great Russians, and others. Minority populations are greatest in Transylvania and the Banat, areas in the north and west, which belonged to the Austro-Hungarian Empire until World War I. Even before union with Romania, ethnic Romanians comprised the overall majority in Transylvania. However, ethnic Hungarians and Germans were the dominant urban population until relatively recently, and still are the majority in a few districts.

Before World War II, minorities represented more than 28% of the total population. During the war that percentage was halved, largely by the loss of the border areas of Bessarabia and northern Bukovina (to the former Soviet Union — now Moldova and Ukraine) and southern Dobrudja (to Bulgaria), as well as by the postwar flight or deportation of ethnic Germans. Though Romanian troops participated in the destruction of the Jewish communities of Bessarabia and Bukovina, many Jews from Romania survived the Holocaust. Mass emigration, mostly to Israel, has reduced the surviving Jewish community from over 300,000 to less than 15,000. In recent years, more than two-thirds of the ethnic Germans in Romania have emigrated to Germany.

Religious affiliation tends to follow ethnic lines, with most ethnic Romanians identifying with the Romanian Orthodox Church. The Greek Catholic or Uniate church, reunified with the Orthodox Church by fiat in 1948, was restored after the 1989 revolution. The 1992 census indicates that 1% of the population is Greek Catholic, as opposed to about 10% prior to 1948. Roman Catholics, largely ethnic Hungarians and Germans, constitute about 5% of the population; Calvinists, Baptists, Pentecostals, and Lutherans make up another 5%. There are smaller numbers of Unitarians, Muslims, and other religions.

Romania's rich cultural traditions have been nourished by many sources, some of which predate the Roman occupation. The traditional folk arts, including dance, wood carving, ceramics, weaving and embroidery of costumes and household decorations, and fascinating folk music, still flourish in many parts of the country. Despite strong Austrian, German, and especially French influence, many of Romania's great artists, such as the painter Nicolae Grigorescu, the poet Mihai Eminescu, the composer George Enescu, and the sculptor Constantin Brancusi, drew their inspiration from Romanian folk traditions. The country's many Orthodox monasteries, as well as the Transylvanian Catholic and Evangelical Churches, some of which date back to the 13th century, are repositories of artistic treasures. The famous painted monasteries of Bukovina make an important contribution to European architecture. Poetry and the theater play an important role in contemporary Romanian life. Classic Romanian plays, such as those of Ion

Luca Caragiale, as well as works by modern or avant-garde Romanian and international playwrights, find sophisticated and enthusiastic audiences in the many theaters of the capital and of the smaller cities.

History of Romania

From about 200 B.C., when it was settled by the Dacians, a Thracian tribe, Romania has been on the path of a series of migrations and conquests. Under the emperor Trajan early in the second century A.D., Dacia was incorporated into the Roman Empire, but was abandoned by a declining Rome less than two centuries later. Romania disappeared from recorded history for hundreds of years, to reemerge in the medieval period as the Principalities of Moldavia and Wallachia. Heavily taxed and badly administered under the Ottoman Empire, the two Principalities were unified under a single native prince in 1859, and had their full independence ratified in the 1878 Treaty of Berlin. A German prince, Carol of Hohenzollern, was crowned first King of Romania in 1881.

The new state, squeezed between the Ottoman, Austro-Hungarian, and Russian empires, with Slav neighbors on three sides, looked to the West, particularly France, for its cultural, educational, and administrative models. Romania was an ally of the Entente and the U.S. in World War I, and was granted sub-

stantial territories with Romanian populations, nota-
bly Transylvania, Bessarabia, and Bukovina, after the
war.

Most of Romania's pre-World War II governments
maintained the forms, but not the substance, of a
liberal constitutional monarchy. The quasi-mystical
fascist Iron Guard movement, exploiting national-
ism, fear of communism, and resentment of alleged
foreign and Jewish domination of the economy, was a
key factor in the creation of a dictatorship in 1938. In
1940-41, the authoritarian General Antonescu took
control. Romania entered World War II on the side of
the Axis Powers in June 1941, invading the Soviet
Union to recover Bessarabia and Bukovina, which had
been annexed in 1940. In August 1944, a coup led by
King Michael, with support from opposition politi-
cians and the army, deposed the Antonescu dictatorship and put Romania's battered armies on the side of
the Allies. Romania incurred additional heavy casual-
ties fighting the Germans in Transylvania, Hungary,
and Czechoslovakia. The peace treaty, signed at Paris
on February 10, 1947, confirmed the Soviet annex-
ation of Bessarabia and northern Bukovina, but restored the part of northern Transylvania granted to
Hungary in 1940 by Hitler. The treaty required mas-
sive war reparations by Romania to the Soviet Union,
whose occupying forces left in 1958. The Soviets
pressed for inclusion of Romania's heretofore negli-

gible Communist Party in the post-war government, while non-communist political leaders were steadily eliminated from political life. King Michael abdicated under pressure in December 1947, when the Romanian People's Republic was declared, and went into exile. In the early 1960s, Romania's communist government began to assert some independence from the Soviet Union. Nicolae Ceausescu became head of the Communist Party in 1965 and head of state in 1967. Ceausescu's denunciation of the 1968 Soviet invasion of Czechoslovakia and a brief relaxation in internal repression helped give him a positive image both at home and in the West. Seduced by Ceausescu's "independent" foreign policy, Western leaders were slow to turn against a regime that, by the late 1970s, had become increasingly harsh, arbitrary, and capricious. Rapid economic growth fueled by foreign credits gradually gave way to wrenching austerity and severe political repression.

After the collapse of communism in the rest of Eastern Europe in the late summer and fall of 1989, a mid-December protest in Timisoara against the forced relocation of a Hungarian minister grew into a country-wide protest against the Ceausescu regime, sweeping the dictator from power. Ceausescu and his wife were executed on December 25, 1989, after a cursory military trial. About 1,500 people were killed in confused street fighting. An impromptu governing coalition, the National Salvation Front (FSN), installed itself and proclaimed the restoration of democracy and freedom. The Communist Party was outlawed, and Ceausescu's most unpopular measures, such as bans on abortion and contraception, were repealed. Ion Iliescu, a former Communist Party official demoted by Ceausescu in the 1970s, emerged as the leader of the FSN. The new government made a crucial early misstep. Unhappy at the continued political and economic influence of members of the Ceausescu-era elite, anti-Communist protesters camped in University Square in April 1990. When miners from the Jiu Valley descended on Bucharest two months later and brutally dispersed the remaining "hooligans," President Iliescu expressed public thanks, thus convincing many that the government had sponsored the miners' actions. His government fell in late September 1991, when the miners returned to Bucharest to demand higher salaries and better living conditions.

Romania has made great progress in consolidating democratic institutions. The press is free and outspoken. Independent radio networks have proliferated, and a private television network now operates nationwide. The reorganized security services have a much reduced role in civil society, but still maintain sole control over the secret police files of the former Communist regime.

Statue of Mátyás Corvinus, Cluj-Napoca

1

"Dracula's Castle, " Bran, Transylvania

2

Peleş Castle, Sinaia, Transylvania

3

Hints on Pronunciation

All the words and phrases are written in a spelling which you read like English. Each letter or combination of letters is used for the sound it normally represents in English and it *always* stands for the same sound. Thus, *oo* is always to be read as in *too, boot, tooth, roost.* Say these words and then pronounce the vowel sound by itself. That is the sound you must use every time you see *oo* in the Pronunciation column. If you should use some other sound—for example, the one in *blood* or the one in *door*—you might be misunderstood.

Syllables that are accented, that is, pronounced louder than others, are written in capital letters. Curved lines (‿) are used to show sounds that are pro-

Babele, or "Old Woman" Rock, Carpathian Mountains

4

nounced together without any break. Example: "BOO-na S‿YA-ra" meaning "good evening."

SPECIAL POINTS

AY as in *day, play, may* but cut short. It may therefore sound something like the *e* in *let.* Example: "PESH-tay" meaning "fish."

U *or* UH as in *cut, but, huh.* Example: "KUT" meaning "how much."

A *or* AH as in *father, ah, pa.* Examples: "DA" meaning "yes," "SHAHP-tay" meaning "seven."

ạ as in *sofa, vanilla, china.* Example: "NO-wạ" meaning "nine."

Church of the Three Hierarchs, Iasi

J for the sound in *measure, usual, division.* Since we have no single letter for this sound in English, we write it in your Language Guide as *j*. Remember that it is like the sound in *measure* and not like the sound in *judge.* Example: "JOY" meaning "Thursday."

y In a word like "kar-TOAF$_y$" the "f" is followed by a slight "y" sound.

Detail, Patriarchate Church, Bucharest

Vlad Ţepeş' House, Sighişoara

GREETINGS AND GENERAL PHRASES

English	Pronunciation	Romanian
Hello	no-ROAK	Noroc
Good day	BOO-nɑ ZEE-wa	Bună ziua

7

English	Pronunciation	Romanian
English	*Pronunciation*	*Romanian*
Good morning	BOO-nǫ dee-meen-YA-tsa	Bună dimineața
Good evening	BOO-nǫ S_YA-ra	Bună seara
Sir	DOAM-noo-lay	Domnule
Mr.	DOAM-nool	Domnul
Mrs.	DWAHM-na	Doamna
Miss	doam-nee-SHWA-ra	Domnișoara
How are you?	chay MA-ee FA-chets?	Ce mai faceți?
I'm well, thanks	mool-tsoo-MESK, BEE-nay	Mulțumesc, bine

Atheneum, Bucharest

English	Pronunciation	Romanian
Thank you	mool-tsoo-MESK	Mulţumesc
You're welcome	PEN-troo poo-TSEEN	Pentru puţin
Please	vǫ ROAG	Vă rog
Excuse me	yayr-TA-tsee-mǫ	Iertaţi-mă
Yes	DA	Da
No	NOO	Nu
Do you understand me?	mun-tsay-LED-jets?	Mă'nţelegeţi?
I understand	un-tsay-LEG	Inţeleg
I don't understand	NOO un-tsay-LEG	Nu înţeleg
Please speak slowly	vǫ ROAG vor-BEETS un-CHET	Vă rog vorbiţi încet
Please repeat	vǫ ROAG ray-pay-TAHTS,	Vă rog repetaţi

LOCATION

When you need directions to get somewhere you use the phrase "where is" and then add the words you need.

9

Calimanesti, on the Olt River

English	Pronunciation	Romanian
Where is ___?	OON-day YEST-ay ___?	Unde este ___?
a restaurant	oon rest-ow-RAHNT	un restaurant
Where is a restaurant?	OON-day YEST-ay oon rest-ow-RAHNT?	Unde este un restaurant?
a hotel	oon ho-TEL	un hotel
Where is a hotel?	OON-day YEST-ay oon ho-TEL?	Unde este un hotel?
the railroad station	GA-ra	gara
Where is the railroad station?	OON-day YEST-ay GA-ra?	Unde este gara?

English	Pronunciation	Romanian
the toilet	la-TREE-na	latrina
Where is the toilet?	OON-day YEST-ay la-TREE-na?	Unde este latrina?

DIRECTIONS

The answer to your question "Where is such and such?" may be "To the right" or "To the left" or "Straight ahead," so you need to know these phrases.

To the right	la dree-AHP-ta	La dreapta
To the left	la STUNG-ga	La stânga
Straight ahead	DREPT un-ah-EEN-tay	Drept înainte

It is sometimes useful to say "Please point" or "Take me there."

Please point	vą ROAG ah-rą-TA-tseem,	Vă rog arătați-mi

Palace of Mogosoaia, Bucharest

11

English	Pronunciation	Romanian
Take me there	koan-doo-CHETS-ee-mặ ah-KO-lo	Conduceţi-mă acolo

If you are driving and ask the distance to another town it will be given you in kilometers, not miles.

| Kilometers | keel-o-MET-ree | Kilometri |

One kilometer equals ⅝ of a mile.

NUMBERS

You need to know the numbers.

One	OO-noo	unu
Two	DOY	doi
Three	TRAY	trei
Four	PA-troo	patru
Five	CHEENCH	cinci
Six	SHA-say	şase
Seven	SHAHP-tay	şapte
Eight	OAPT	opt
Nine	NO-wặ	nouă
Ten	ZECH-ay	zece

Culture Palace, Târgu Mureş, Transylvania

13

English	Pronunciation	Romanian
Eleven	OON-spray-ZECH-ay	unsprezece
Twelve	DOY-spray-ZECH-ay	doisprezece
Thirteen	TRAY-spray-ZECH-ay	treisprezece
Fourteen	PA-ee-spray-ZECH-ay	paisprezece
Fifteen	CHEENCH-spray-ZECH-ay	cincisprezece
Sixteen	SHA-ee-spray-ZECH-ay	şaisprezece
Seventeen	SHAHP-tay- pray-ZECH-ay	şaptesprezece
Eighteen	OAPT-spray-ZECH-ay	optsprezece
Nineteen	NO-wą-spray-ZECH-ay	nouăsprezece
Twenty	DO-wą-ZECH	douăzeci
Twenty-one	do-wą-ZECH shee OO-noo	douăzeci şi unu
Twenty-two	do-wą-ZECH shee DOY	douăzeci şi doi

English	Pronunciation	Romanian
Thirty	tray-ZECH	treizeci
Forty	PA-troo-ZECH	patruzeci
Fifty	cheench-ZECH	cincizeci
Sixty	SHA-ee-ZECH	şaizeci
Seventy	SHAHP-tay-ZECH	şaptezeci
Eighty	oapt-ZECH	optzeci
Ninety	NO-wą-ZECH	nouăzeci
One hundred	o SOO-tą	o sută
One thousand	o MEE-yay	o mie

WHAT'S THIS?

When you want to know the name of something you can say "What is it?" or "What's this?" and point to the thing you mean.

What is ___?	CHAY YEST-ay ___?	Ce este ___?
this	AH-sta	asta
What's this?	CHAY YEST-ay AH-sta?	Ce este asta?

15

ASKING FOR THINGS

When you want something, you can say "I'd like" and add the name of the thing wanted.

I'd like ___	ahsh vree-AH ___	Aş vrea ___
cigarettes	tsee-ga-RET-ay	ţigarete
I'd like cigarettes	ahsh vree-AH tsee-ga-RET-ay	Aş vrea ţigarete

| to eat | sǫ   mǫ-NUNK | să mănânc |
| I'd like to eat | ahsh   vree-AH sǫ   mǫ-NUNK | Aş vrea să mănânc |

Give me ___	DA-tseem_y ___	Daţi-mi ___
a match	oon kee-BREET	un chibrit
Give me a match	DA-tseem_y oon kee-BREET	Daţi-mi un chibrit

Always add the word for "please"—"vǫ ROAG."

| I'd like to buy ___ | ahsh   vree-AH sǫ   KOOM- pur ___ | Aş vrea să cumpăr ___ |

Here are the words for some of the things you may require.

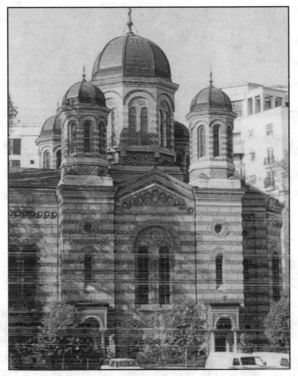

St. Apostles' Church, Bucharest

English	Pronunciation	Romanian
food	day mun-KA-ray	de mâncare
bread	PWEE-nay	pâine
butter	OONT	unt

English	Pronunciation	Romanian
water	AH-pₐ	apă
soup	SOO-pₐ	supă
fish	PESH-tay	peşte
meat	KAR-nay	carne
chicken	poo-EE	pui
vegetables	lay-GOO-may	legume
eggs	O-wₐ	ouă
salt	SA-ray	sare
sugar	ZA-hur	zahăr
pepper	pee-PAYR	piper
potatoes	kar-TOAF𝔂	cartofi

Constanta, on the Black Sea

Notice the last sound in the word for "potatoes." Listen and repeat: "kar-TOAF$_y$, kar-TOAF$_y$." It is written in your Guide as *f* with a small *y* following it. It is pronounced like *f* and *y* run together in one sound; it is the same sound we have in the words "few" and "future." Try just the sound again: "f$_y$, f$_y$."

beans	fa-SO-lay	fasole
milk	LAHP-tay	lapte
chocolate	cho-ko-LA-tạ	ciocolată
tea	CHA-ee	ceaiu
wine	VEEN	vin
cup of coffee	CHA-shkạ day kahf-YA	ceașcă de cafea
glass of beer	pa-HAR day BAY-ray	pahar de bere

MONEY

To find out how much things cost you say "How much costs?"

how much	KUT	cât
costs	KO-stạ	costă
this	AH-sta	asta

19

English	Pronunciation	Romanian
How much does this cost?	KUT KO-stą AH-sta?	Cât costă asta?

Notice the sound written with a *u* in the word "KUT, KUT." It sounds something like *u* in "cut." Try just the sound again: "u, u."

TIME

To find out what time it is you say really "What is the hour?"

What time is it?	KUT YEST-ay CHA-sool?	Cât este ceasul?
It's one o'clock	YEST-ay CHA-sool OO-noo	Este ceasul unu

"Half past four" is "four and a half."

Half past four	PA-troo shee joo-mą-TA-tay	Patru şi jumătate

WHAT TIME IS IT IN ROMANIAN?

Cluj, Transylvania

If you want to know when a movie starts or when a train leaves you say:

when	KUND	când
starts	un-CHEP-ay	începe
the movie	FEEL-mool	filmul
When does the movie start?	KUND un-CHEP-ay FEEL-mool?	Când începe filmul?
leaves	plee-AH-kₐ	pleacă
the train	TREN-ool	trenul
When does the train leave?	KUND plee-AH-kₐ TREN-ool?	Când pleacă trenul?

English	Pronunciation	Romanian
Yesterday	YAYR$_y$	Ieri
Today	AHZ$_y$	Azi
Tomorrow	MWEE-nay	Mâine

The days of the week are:

Monday	LOON$_y$	Luni
Tuesday	MARTS$_y$	Marţi
Wednesday	M‿YAYR-koor$_y$	Miercuri
Thursday	JOY	Joi

Notice the sound written with a *j* in the word "JOY, JOY." It is the same as the sound in "measure," "pleasure." Try just the sound again: "j, j."

Friday	VEE-nayr$_y$	Vineri
Saturday	SUM-but-q	Sâmbătă
Sunday	doo-MEE-nay-kq	Duminecă

OTHER USEFUL PHRASES

The following phrases will be useful:

What is your name?	koom vq noo-MEETS$_y$?	Cum vă numiţi?

English	Pronunciation	Romanian
How do you say "table" (*or anything else*) in Romanian?	KOOM say SPOO-nay "table" pay ro-mᶐ-NESH-tay?	Cum se spune "table" pe românește?
I am American	SOONT ah-may-ree-KAHN	Sunt american
Good-by	LA rev-ay-DAY-ray	La revedere

NOTES: For "cigarettes" you will often hear the word "tsee-GUR" as well as "tsee-ga-RET-ay."

You can shorten the expression for "It's one o'clock" (and so forth) by leaving out the word for "hour" and saying simply "YEST-ay OO-noo."

All Saints' Church, Chişinău, Moldova

23

ADDITIONAL EXPRESSIONS

Come in!	EEN-trą!	Intră!
Have a seat!	LWAHTS LOAK!	Luaţi loc!
Glad to meet you!	UM PA-ra BEE-nay!	Îmi pare bine!
I don't know	NOO sht‿yoo	Nu ştiu
I think so	KRED	Cred
I don't think so	NOO KRED	Nu cred
Maybe	PWA-tay	Poate
Stop!	STA-ee!	Stai!
Come here!	vay-NEETS ah-CHEE!	Veniţi aci!
Right away! *or* Quickly!	REP-ed-ay!	Repede!
Come quickly!	vay-NEETS REP-ed-ay!	Veniţi repede!
Go quickly!	doo-CHETS-ee-vą REP-ed-ay!	Duceţi-vă repede!
I am hungry	MEE-yay FWA-may	Mi-e foame

Sucevita Monastery

English	Pronunciation	Romanian
I am thirsty	MEE-yay SET-ay	Mi-e sete
I am tired	SOONT o-bo-SEET	Sunt obosit
I am lost	MAHM rut-a-CHEET	M'am rătăcit
Help!	ah-joo-TOR!	Ajutor!
Help me	ah-joo-TA-tsee-ma	Ajutați-mă
Bring help	ah-DOO-chets ah-joo-TOR	Aduceți ajutor
I will pay you	va VOY pla-TEE	Vă voiu plăti

English	Pronunciation	Romanian
Where is a town or city?	OON-day YEST-ay oon SAHT or o-RAHSH?	Unde este un sat ori oraş?
Where is it?	OON-day YEST-ay?	Unde este?
How far is the city?	KUT day day-PAR-tay yest-ay o-RA-shool?	Cât de departe este oraşul?
Is it far?	YEST-ay day-PAR-tay?	Este departe?
Is it near?	YEST-ay ah-PRWA-pay?	Este aproape?
How far is it?	KUT day day-PAR-tay YEST-ay?	Cât de departe este?
Which way is north?	un CHAY dee-REKTS-yay yest-ay NOR-dool?	În ce direcţie este nordul?
Which is the road to ___?	KA-ray YEST-ay DROO-mool spray ___?	Care este drumul spre ___?

English	Pronunciation	Romanian
Draw me a map	FA-chets o SKEE-tsą	Faceţi o schiţă
Take me there	koan-doo-CHETS-ee-mą ah-KO-lo	Conduceţi-mă acolo
Take me to a doctor	koan-doo-CHETS-ee-mą la oon DOAK-tor	Conduceţi-mă la un doctor
Take me to the hospital	doo-CHETS-ee-mą la spee-TAHL	Duceţi-mă la spital
Danger!	pay-REE-koal!	Pericol!
Watch out!	ah-TENTS-yay!	Atenţie!

Court of Arges, Bucharest

27

The Russian Church, Bucharest

English	Pronunciation	Romanian
English	*Pronunciation*	*Romanian*
Wait a minute!	ahsh-tep-TAHTS poo-TSEEN!	Aşteptaţi puţin!
Good luck!	no-ROAK!	Noroc!

FILL-IN SENTENCES

In this section you will find a number of sentences, each containing a blank space which can be filled in with any one of the words in the list that follows. For example, if you want to say "Where can I find soap?" look for the sentence for "Where can I find ___?" and, in the list following the sentence, the word for "soap." You then combine the words as shown here:

Where can I find ___?	OON-day poat ga-SEE ___?	Unde pot găsi ___?
soap	sa-POON	săpun
Where can I find soap?	OON-day poat ga-SEE sa POON?	Unde pot găsi săpun?

I want ___	ahsh vree-AH ___	Aş vrea ___
We want ___	ahm vree-AH ___	Am vrea ___
Give me ___	DA-tseem ___	Daţi-mi ___
Bring me ___	ah-doo-CHETS-eem ___	Aduceţi-mi ___
Where can I find ___?	OON-day poat ga-SEE ___?	Unde pot găsi ___?

English	Pronunciation	Romanian
I have ___	AHM ___	Am ___
We have ___	ah-VEM ___	Avem ___
We don't have ___	noo ah-VEM ___	Nu avem ___
Have you ___?	ah-VETS ___?	Aveți ___?

EXAMPLE

I want ___	ahsh vree-AH ___	Aş vrea ___
food	day mun-KA-ray	de mâncare
I want food	ahsh vree-AH day mun-KA-ray	Aş vrea de mâncare

apples	MAY-ray	mere
boiled water	AH-p*q* F⌣YAR-t*q*	apă fiartă
cabbage	VAR-z*q*	varză
carrots	MOR-koav	morcovi
cornmeal mush	mum-*q*-LEE-g*q*	mămăligă
drinking water	AH-p*q* day b*q*-OOT	apă de băut
fruit	FROOK-tay	fructe
onions	CHA-'p*q*	ceapă

English	Pronunciation	Romanian
pears	PAY-ray	pere
spinach	spa-NAHK	spanac
a cup	o CHA-shkᵩ	o ceaşcă
a fork	o foor-koo-LEE-tsᵩ	o furculiţă
a glass	oon pa-HAR	un pahar
a knife	oon koo-TSEET	un cuţit
a plate	o far-foo-REE-yay	o farfurie
a spoon	o LEEN-goo-rᵩ	o lingură
a bed	oon PAHT	un pat
blankets	PUTT-oo-ree	pături
mattress	sahlt-YA	saltea
a mosquito net	o rets-YA koan-tra tsun-TSA-ree-lor	o reţea contra ţânţarilor
a pillow	o PAYR-nᵩ	o pernă
a room	o KA-may-rᵩ	o cameră
sheets	chayr-CHA-foor	cerceafuri

31

English	Pronunciation	Romanian
cigars	tsee-GUR day FOY	ţigări de foi
a pipe	o PEE-pǫ	o pipă
tobacco	too-TOON	tutun
ink	chayrn-YA-lǫ	cerneală
paper	hur-TEE-yay	hârtie
a pen	oon koan-DAY	un condeiu
a pencil	oon kray-YOAN	un creion
a comb	oon P‿YEP-ten-ay	un pieptene
hot water	AH-pǫ f‿yayr-BEEN-tay	apă fierbinte
a razor	o ma-SHEE-nǫ day RAHSS	o maşină de ras
razor blades	LA-may day RAHSS	lame de ras
a shaving brush	oon pum-ǫ-TOOF day RAHSS	un pămătuf de ras
soap	sǫ-POON	săpun
shaving soap	sǫ-POON day RAHSS	săpun de ras

English	Pronunciation	Romanian
a tooth-brush	o payr-YOO-tsɑ day DEENTS	o periuţă de dinţi
toothpaste	PA-stɑ day DEENTS	pastă de dinţi
a towel	oon pro-SOAP	un prosop
a hand-kerchief	o ba-TEE-stɑ	o batistă
a raincoat	o mahn-TA day PLWA-yay	o manta de ploaie
a shirt	o kɑ-MA-shɑ	o cămaşă
shoes	GET-ay	ghete
shoe laces	shee-RET-oor day GET-ay	şireturi de ghete
shoe polish	KREM-ɑ day GET-ay	cremă de ghete
an under-shirt	o fla-NEL-ɑ	o flanelă
under-shorts	een-dee-spen-SA-beel	indispensabili
buttons	NA-stoor	nasturi
a needle	oon AHK	un ac
safety pins	AH-chay day see-goo-RAHN-tsɑ	ace de siguranţă

WHICH IS WHICH?

SOAP

TOOTHBRUSH

sa-POON
oon pro-SOAP
o ma-SHEE-na day RAHSS
o payr-YOO-tsa day DEENTS

RAZOR

TOWEL

34   *(Answers in Word List)*

English	Pronunciation	Romanian
thread	AH-ts*q*	aţă
adhesive tape	PLA-stroo	plastru
an anti-septic	oon ahn-tee-sep-TEEK	un antiseptic
aspirin	ah-spee-REE-n*q*	aspirină
a bandage	oon bahn-DAHJ	un bandaj
cotton	VA-t*q*	vată
a dis-infectant	oon day-zeen-fek-TAHNT	un desinfectant
iodine	YOAD	iod
a laxative	oon lahk-sa-TEEV	un laxativ
a bicycle	o bee-chee-KLET-*q*	o bicicletă
gasoline	ben-ZEE-n*q*	benzină
I want to ___	ahsh vree-AH s*q* ___	Aş vrea să ___

EXAMPLE

I want to ___	ahsh vree-AH s*q* ___	Aş vrea să ___

35

English	Pronunciation	Romanian
eat	mₐ-NUNK	mănânc
I want to eat	ahsh vree-AH sₐ mₐ-NUNK	Aş vrea să mănânc
be shaved	mₐ RAHD	mă rad
drink	B‿YOW	beau
have my clothes washed	DOW HA-ee-nel-ay la spₐ-LAHT	dau hainele la spălat
have my hair cut	mₐ TOOND	mă tund
pay	plₐ-TESK	plătesc
rest	mₐ o-deeh-NESK	mă odihnesc
sleep	DORM	dorm
take a bath	FAHK o BA-ay	fac o bae
wash up	mₐ SPUL	mă spăl

Where is ___?	OON-day YEST-ay ___?	Unde este ___?

EXAMPLE

Where can I find ___?	OON-day poat gŭ-SEE ___?	Unde pot găsi ___
Where is ___?	OON-day YEST-ay ___?	Unde este ___?
a barber	oon burb-YAYR	un bărbier
Where is a barber?	OON-day YEST-ay oon burb-YAYR?	Unde este un bărbier?
a dentist	oon den-TEEST	un dentist
a doctor	oon DOAK-tor	un doctor
a mechanic	oon may-KA-neek	un mecanic
a policeman	oon gar-DEEST	un gardist
a porter	oon ha-MAHL	un hamal
a shoe-maker	oon cheez-MAR	un cizmar
a tailor	oon kroy-TOR	un croitor
a workman	oon loo-krŭ-TOR	un lucrător
a church	o bee-SAY-ree-kŭ	o biserică
a clothing store	oon ma-ga-ZEEN day HA-ee-nay	un magazin de haine

English	Pronunciation	Romanian
a drug-store *or* pharmacy	o far-ma-CHEE-yay	o farmacie
a filling station	o STAHTS-yay day ben-ZEE-n*a*	o stație de benzină
a garage	oon ga-RAHJ	un garaj
a grocery store	o buk-*a*-NEE-yay	o băcănie
a house	o KA-s*a*	o casă
a laundry	o spul-ut-o-REE-ay	o spălătorie
a pump (*for water*)	o cheesh-M⌣YA	o cișmea
a spring	oon eez-VOR	un izvor
a well	o fun-TUN-*a*	o fântână
the bus	out-o-BOO-zool	autobusul
the camp	TA-bur-ah	tabăra
the city	o-RA-shool	orașul

English	Pronunciation	Romanian
the high-way	DROO-mool preen-chee-PAHL	drumul principal
the hospital	spee-TA-lool	spitalul
the main street	STRA-da preen-chee-PA-lᴧ	strada principală
the market	pee-YA-tsa	piaţa
the nearest town *or* city	chel MA-ee ah-proap-YAHT SAHT or o-RAHSH	cel mai apropiat sat ori oraş
the police station	po-LEETS-ya	poliţia
the post office	PO-shta	poşta
the rail-road	KAHL-ya fay-RA-tᴧ	calea ferată
the river	RUH-ool	râul
the road	DROO-mool	drumul
the street-car	trahm-VA-yool	tramvaiul
the tele-graph office	o-FEECH-ool tel-eg-RA-feek	oficiul telegrafic

39

English	Pronunciation	Romanian
the telephone	tel-ay-FO-nool	telefonul
the town	SA-tool	satul

English	Pronunciation	Romanian
I am ___	SOONT ___	Sunt ___
He is ___	YEST-ay ___	Este ___

EXAMPLE

English	Pronunciation	Romanian
I am ___	SOONT ___	Sunt ___
an American	ah-may-ree-KAHN	american
I am an American	SOONT ah-may-ree-KAHN	Sunt american

English	Pronunciation	Romanian
sick	boal-NAHV	bolnav
tired	o-bo-SEET	obosit
wounded	r*a*-NEET	rănit

English	Pronunciation	Romanian
We are ___	soon-TEM ___	Suntem ___
They are ___	YAY SOONT ___	Ei sunt ___
Are you ___?	soon-TETS ___?	Sunteţi ___?

40

WHICH IS WHICH?

BANDAGE

BRIDGE

POAD
KAHL-ya fay-RA-ta
tel-uy-FOAN
bahn-DAHJ

RAILROAD

TELEPHONE

(Answers in Word List)

We are ___	soon-TEM ___	Suntem ___
Amer- icans	ah-may-ree-KAHN	americani
We are Americans	soon-TEM ah- may-ree-KAHN	Suntem americani
sick	boal-NAHV	bolnavi
tired	o-bo-SEETS	obosiţi
wounded	ra-NEETS	răniţi

Is it ___?	YEST-ay ___?	Este ___?
It is ___	YEST-ay ___	Este ___
It is not ___	NOO YEST- ay ___	Nu este ___
This is ___ or That is ___	AH-sta YEST- ay ___	Asta este ___
It is too ___	YEST-ay pree- AH ___	Este prea ___
It is very ___	YEST-ay FWAR-tay ___	Este foarte ___

It is not ___	NOO YEST-ay ___	Nu este ___
cold	FREEG	frig
It is not cold	NOO YEST-ay FREEG	Nu este frig

warm	KAHLD	cald
clean	koo-RAHT	curat
dirty	moor-DAR	murdar
cheap	YEF-teen	eftin
expensive	SKOOMP	scump
large	MA-ray	mare
small	MEEK	mic
much	MOOLT	mult
enough	dess-TOOL	destul
bad	PROAST	prost
good	BOON	bun
here	ah-CHEE	aci
there	ah-KO-lo	acolo
near	ah-PRWA-pay	aproape
far	day-PAR-tay	departe

43

IMPORTANT SIGNS

Stop	Stop
La pas	Go Slow
Circulaţie pe variantă	Detour
Atenţie	Caution
Pericol	Danger

Hunedoaṛa Castle, Transylvania

Romanian	English
Sens unic	One Way Street
Trecerea oprită	No Thoroughfare
Fundătură	Dead End
Ţine dreapta	Keep to the Right
Atenţie la cotitură	Dangerous Curve
Cale ferată	Railroad
Pod	Bridge
Incrucişare	Crossroad
Pericol de moarte	Danger of Death (High Tension Lines)
Bărbaţi	Men
Femei	Women
Latrină	Lavatory
Fumatul oprit	No Smoking
Staţionarea interzisă	No Parking
Intrerea oprită	Keep Out
Deschis	Open
Închis	Closed

45

Wooden church, Bucegi Mountains, Transylvania

ALPHABETICAL
WORD LIST

English	*Pronunciation*	*Romanian*
	A	
a *or* an	o *or* oon	o un
adhesive tape	PLA-stroo	plastru
am		
I am ___	SOONT ___	Sunt ___
American		
I am an Amer-ican	SOONT ah-may-ree-KAHN	Sunt american
We are Americans	soon-TEM ah-may-ree-KAHN	Suntem americani
antiseptic	ahn-tee-sep-TEEK	antiseptic
apples	MAY-ray	mere
are		
Are you ___?	soon-TETS ___?	Sunteţi ___?
They are ___	YAY SOONT ___	Ei sunt ___

English	Pronunciation	Romanian
We are __	soon-TEM __	Suntem __
aspirin	ah-spee-REE-nq	aspirină

B

bad	PROAST	prost
bandage	bahn-DAHJ	bandaj
barber	burb-YAYR	bărbier
bath	BA-ay	bae
I want to take a bath	ahsh vree-AH sq FAHK o BA-av	Aş vrea să fac o bae
beans	fa-SO-lay	fasole
bed	PAHT	pat
beer	BAY-ray	bere
glass of beer	pa-HAR day BAY-ray	pahar de bere
bicycle	bee-chee-KLET-q	bicicletă
blades		
razor blades	LA-may day RAHSS	lame de ras

48

English	Pronunciation	Romanian
blankets	PUTT-oo-ree	pături
boiled water	AH-pą F‿YAR-tą	apă fiartă
bread	PWEE-nay	pâine
bridge	POAD	pod
the bridge	PO-dool	podul
bring		
Bring help	ah-DOO-chets ah-joo-TOR	Aduceţi ajutor
Bring me	ah-doo-CHETS-eem ___	Aduceţi-mi ___
brush		
shaving brush	pum-ą-TOOF day RAHSS	pămătuf de ras
toothbrush	payr-YOO-tsą day DEENTS	periuţă de dinţi
bus	out-o-BOOZ	autobus
the bus	out-o-BOO-zool	autobusul
butter	OONT	unt
buttons	NA-stoor	nasturi

49

English	Pronunciation	Romanian
buy		
I'd like to buy ___	ahsh vree-AH sq KOOM-pur ___	Aş vrea să cumpăr ___

C

cabbage	VAR-zq	varză
camp	TA-bur-q	tabără
the camp	TA-bur-ah	tabăra
carrots	MOR-koav	morcovi
cheap	YEF-teen	eftin
chicken	poo-EE	pui

Royal Summer residence, Bucharest

50

English	Pronunciation	Romanian
chocolate	cho-ko-LA-t*a*	ciocolată
church	bee-SAY-ree-k*a*	biserică
cigarettes	tsee-ga-RET-ay *or* tsee-GUR	ţigarete ţigări
cigars	tsee-GUR day FOY	ţigări de foi
city	o-RAHSH	oraş
the city	o-RA-shool	oraşul
clean	koo-RAHT	curat
clothes		
I want to have my clothes washed	ahsh vree-AH s*a* DOW HA-ee-nel-ay la sp*a*-LAHT	Aş vrea să dau hainele la spălat
clothing store	ma-ga-ZEEN day HA-ee-nay	magazin de haine
coffee	kahf-YA	cafea
cup of coffee	CHA-shk*a* day kahf-YA	ceaşcă de cafea
cold (*weather*)	FREEG	frig
comb	P‿YEP-ten-ay	pieptene

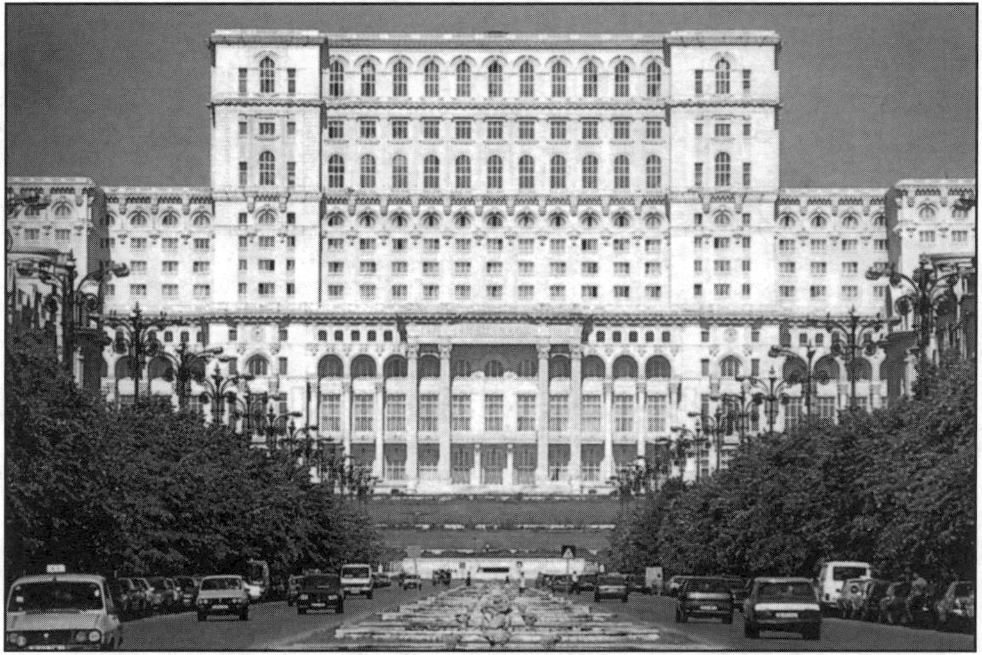

The Palace of Parliament from B-dul Unirii, Bucharest

Piaţa Mare, Sibiu, Transylvania

53

English	Pronunciation	Romanian
come		
Come here!	vay-NEETS ah-CHEE!	Veniți aci!
Come in!	EEN-trą!	Intră!
Come quickly!	vay-NEETS REP-ed-ay!	Veniți repede!
cornmeal mush	mum-ą-LEE-gą	mămăligă
cost		
How much does this cost?	KUT KO-stą AH-sta?	Cât costă asta?
cotton	VA-tą	vată
cup	CHA-shką	ceașcă
cup of coffee	CHA-shką day kahf-YA	ceașcă de cafea

D

Danger!	pay-REE-koal!	Pericol!
day		
Good day	BOO-ną ZEE-wa	Bună ziua

54

English	Pronunciation	Romanian
dentist	den-TEEST	dentist
dirty	moor-DAR	murdar
disinfectant	day-zeen-fek-TAHNT	desinfectant
doctor	DOAK-tor	doctor
Take me to a doctor	koan-doo-CHETS-ee-mᶐ la oon DOAK-tor	Conduceți-mă la un doctor
Draw me a map	FA-chets o SKEE-tsᶐ	Faceți o schiță
drink		
I want to drink	ahsh vree AH sᶐ B‿YOW	Aş vrea să beau
drinking water	AH-pᶐ day bᶐ-OOT	apă de băut
drug store	far-ma-CHEE-yay	farmacie

E

eat		
I want to eat	ahsh vree-AH sᶐ mᶐ-NUNK	Aş vrea să mănânc
eggs	O-wᶐ	ouă

55

WHICH IS WHICH?

BUTTER

BREAD

PWEE-nay
PAHT
kahf-YA
OONT

BED

COFFEE

(Answers in Word List)

English	Pronunciation	Romanian
English	*Pronunciation*	*Romanian*
eight	OAPT	opt
eighteen	OAPT-spray-ZECH-ay	optsprezece
eighty	oapt-ZECH	optzeci
eleven	OON-spray-ZECH-ay	unsprezece
enough	dess-TOOL	destul
evening		
Good evening	BOO-nø S_YA-ra	Bună seara
Excuse me	yayr-TA-tsee-mø	Iertați-mă
expensive	SKOOMP	scump

F

far	day-PAR-tay	departe
How far is the city?	KUT day day-PAR-tay yest-ay o-RA-shool?	Cât de departe este orașul?
How far is it?	KUT day day-PAR-tay YEST-ay?	Cât de departe este?

English	Pronunciation	Romanian
Is it far?	YEST-ay day-PAR-tay?	Este departe?
fifteen	CHEENCH-spray-ZECH-ay	cincisprezece
fifty	cheench-ZECH	cincizeci
filling station	STAHTS-yay day ben-ZEE-nø	stație de benzină
find		
Where can I find ___?	OON-day poat gø-SEE ___?	Unde pot găsi ___?
fish	PESH-tay	peşte
five	CHEENCH	cinci
food	day mun-KA-ray	de mâncare
fork	foor-koo-LEE-tsø	furculiță
forty	PA-troo-ZECH	patruzeci
four	PA-troo	patru
fourteen	PA-ee-spray-ZECH-ay	paisprezece
Friday	VEE-nayrᵧ	Vineri
fruit	FROOK-tay	fructe

58

English	Pronunciation	Romanian
	G	
garage	ga-RAHJ	garaj
gasoline	ben-ZEE-nᴗ	benzină
Give me ___	DA-tseem ___	Daţi-mi ___
Glad to meet you!	UM PA-ra BEE-nay!	Îmi pare bine!
glass	pa-HAR	pahar
glass of beer	pa-HAR day BAY-ray	pahar de bere
good	BOON	bun
Good day	BOO-nᴗ ZEE-wa	Bună ziua
Good evening	BOO-nᴗ S⌣YA-ra	Bună seara
Good luck	no-ROAK!	Noroc!
Good morning	BOO-nᴗ dee-meen-YA-tsa	Bună dimineaţa
Good-by	LA rev-ay-DAY-ray	La revedere
Go quickly!	doo-CHETS-ee-vᴗ REP-ed-ay!	Duceţi-vă repede!
grocery store	buk-ᴗ-NEE-yay	băcănie

59

English	Pronunciation	Romanian

H

hair

I want to have my hair cut	ahsh vree-AH să mə TOOND	Aş vrea să mă tund
half	joo-mə-TA-tay	jumătate
half past four	PA-troo shee joo-mə-TA-tay	patru şi jumătate
handkerchief	ba-TEE-stə	batistă

have

I have ___	AHM ___	Am ___
We have ___	ah-VEM ___	Avem ___
We don't have ___	noo ah-VEM ___	Nu avem ___
Have a seat	LWAHTS LOAK	Luaţi loc
Have you ___?	ah-VETS ___?	Aveţi ___?
he	YEL	el
He is ___	YEST-ay ___	Este ___

English	Pronunciation	Romanian
Hello *or* Good luck	no-ROAK	Noroc
Help!	ah-joo-TOR!	Ajutor!
Bring help	ah-DOO-chets ah-joo-TOR	Aduceţi ajutor
Help me	ah-joo-TA-tsee-mǫ	Ajutaţi-mă
here	ah-CHEE	aci
highway	DROOM preen-chee-PAHL	drum principal
the highway	DROO-mool preen-chee-PAHL	drumul principal
hospital	spee-TAHL	spital
the hospital	spee-TA-lool	spitalul
Take me to the hospital	doo-CHETS-ee-mǫ la spee-TAHL	Duceţi-mă la spital
hot water	AH-pǫ f‿yayr-BEEN-tay	apă fierbinte
hotel	ho-TEL	hotel
Where is a hotel?	OON-day YEST-ay oon ho-TEL?	Unde este un hotel?

English	Pronunciation	Romanian
house	KA-sɑ	casă
how		
How are you?	chay MA-ee FA-chets?	Ce mai faceţi?
How do you say ___?	KOOM say SPOO-nay ___?	Cum se spune ___?
How far is it?	KUT day day-PAR-tay YEST-ay?	Cât de departe este?
how much	KUT	cât
How much does this cost?	KUT KO-stɑ AH-sta?	Cât costă asta?
hundred	SOO-tɑ	sută
hungry		
I am hungry	MEE-yay FWA-may	Mi-e foame

I

I	YAY‿oo	eu
I am ___	SOONT ___	Sunt ___

English	Pronunciation	Romanian
I'd like ___ *or* I want ___	ahsh vree-AH ___	Aş vrea ___
I have ___	AHM ___	Am ___
I want to ___	ahsh vree-AH sạ ___	Aş vrea să ___
ink	chayrn-YA-lạ	cerneală
iodine	YOAD	iod
is	YEST-ay	este
it		
It is ___	YEST-ay ___	Este ___
It is not ___	NOO YEST- ay ___	Nu este ___
It is too ___	YEST-ay pree- AH ___	Este prea ___
It is very ___	YEST-ay FWAR-tay ___	Este foarte ___

K

kilometers	keel-o-MET-ree	kilometri
knife	koo-TSEET	cuţit

63

English	Pronunciation	Romanian
know		
I don't know	NOO sht‿yoo	Nu ştiu

L

English	Pronunciation	Romanian
laces		
shoelaces	shee-RET-oor day GET-ay	şireturi de ghete
large	MA-ray	mare
laundry	spul-ut-o-REE-ay	spălătorie
laxative	lahk-sa-TEEV	laxativ
leave		
When does the train leave?	KUND plee-AH-kᶐ TREN-ool?	Când pleacă trenul?
left		
To the left	la STUNG-ga	La stânga
like		
I'd like ___	ahsh vree-AH ___	Aş vrea ___
lost		
I am lost	MAHM rut-ᶐ-CHEET	M'am rătăcit

English	Pronunciation	Romanian
luck		
Good luck!	no-ROAK!	Noroc!

M

English	Pronunciation	Romanian
main street	STRA-dạ preen-chee-PA-lạ	stradă principală
the main street	STRA-da preen-chee-PA-lạ	stradă principală
map	SKEE-tsạ	schiță
Draw me a map	FA-chets o SKEE-tsạ	Faceți o schiță
market	pee-YA-tsạ	piață
the market	pee-YA-tsa	piața
match	kee-BREET	chibrit
mattress	sahlt-YA	saltea
maybe	PWA-tay	poate
meat	KAR-nay	carne
mechanic	may-KA-neek	mecanic
meet		
Glad to meet you!	UM PA-ra BEE-nay!	Îmi pare bine!

English	Pronunciation	Romanian
milk	LAHP-tay	lapte
minute		
Wait a minute!	ahsh-tep-TAHTS poo-TSEEN!	Aşteptaţi puţin!
Miss	doam-nee-SHWA-ra	Domnişoara
Monday	LOON_y	Luni
morning		
Good morning	BOO-nạ dee-meen-YA-tsa	Bună dimineaţa
movie	FEELM	film
the movie	FEEL-mool	filmul

Statue of Hercules, Herculane

English	Pronunciation	Romanian
When does the movie start?	KUND un-CHEP-ay FEEL-mool?	Când începe filmul?
Mr.	DOAM-nool	Domnul
Mrs.	DWAHM-na	Doamna
much	MOOLT	mult
How much?	KUT?	Cât?

N

English	Pronunciation	Romanian
name		
What is your name?	koom vǫ noo-MEETSy?	Cum vă numiți?
near	ah-PRWA-pay	aproape
Is it near?	YEST-ay ah-PRWA-pay?	Este aproape?
the nearest town or city	chel MA-ee ah-proap-YAHT SAHT or o-RAHSH	cel mai apropiat sat ori oraș
needle	AHK	ac
nine	NO-wǫ	nouă

English	Pronunciation	Romanian
nineteen	NO-wą-spray-ZECH-ay	nouăsprezece
ninety	NO-wą-ZECH	nouăzeci
No	NOO	Nu
north	NORD	nord
Which way is north?	un CHAY dee-REKTS-yay yest-ay NOR-dool?	În ce direcţie este nordul?

O

o'clock		
It's one o'clock	YEST-ay CHA-sool OO-noo	Este ceasul unu
	or YEST-ay OO-noo	Este unu
one	OO-noo	unu
onions	CHA-pą	ceapă

P

paper	hur-TEE-yay	hârtie
past		
half past four	PA-troo shee joo-mą-TA-tay	patru şi jumătate

English	Pronunciation	Romanian
pay		
I will pay you	vₐ VOY plₐ-TEE	Vă voiu plăti
I want to pay	ahsh vree-AH sₐ plₐ-TESK	Aş vrea să plătesc
pears	PAY-ray	pere
pen	koan-DAY	condeiu
pencil	kray-YOAN	creion
pepper	pee-PAYR	piper
pillow	PAYR-nₐ	pernă
pins		
safety pins	AH-chay day see-goo-RAHN-tsₐ	ace de siguranţă
pipe	PEE-pₐ	pipă
plate	far-foo-REE-yay	farfurie
Please	vₐ ROAG	Vă rog
Please point	vₐ ROAG ah-rₐ-TA-tseem,	Vă rog arătaţi-mi
point		
Please point	vₐ ROAG ah-rₐ-TA-tseem,	Vă rog arătaţi-mi

69

WHICH IS WHICH?

FRUIT

PENCIL

la-TREEN-na
kray-YOAN
O-wa
FROOK-tay

TOILET

EGGS

(Answers in Word List)

English	Pronunciation	Romanian
policeman	gar-DEEST	gardist
police station	po-LEETS-yay	poliție
the police station	po-LEETS-ya	poliția
polish		
shoe polish	KREM-q day GET-ay	cremă de ghete
porter	ha-MAHL	hamal
post office	PO-shtq	poștă
the post office	PO-shta	poșta
potatoes	kar-TOAF_y	cartofi
pump (*for water*)	cheesh-M⌣YA	cișmea

Q

quickly	REP-ed-ay	repede
Come quickly!	vay-NEETS REP-ed-ay!	Veniți repede!
Go quickly!	doo-CHETS-ee-vq REP-ed-ay!	Duceți-vă repede!

English	Pronunciation	Romanian

R

English	Pronunciation	Romanian
railroad	KA-lay fay-RA-t*ą*	cale ferată
the railroad	KAHL-ya fay-RA-t*ą*	calea ferată
railroad station	GA-r*ą*	gară
the railroad station	GA-ra	gara
Where is the railroad station?	OON-day YEST-ay GA-ra?	Unde este gara?
raincoat	mahn-TA day PLWA-yay	manta de ploaie
razor	ma-SHEE-n*ą* day RAHSS	maşină de ras
razor blades	LA-may day RAHSS	lame de ras
repeat		
Please repeat	v*ą* ROAG ray-pay-TAHTS*y*	Vă rog repetaţi
rest		
I want to rest	ahsh vree-AH s*ą* m*ą* o-deeh-NESK	Aş vrea să mă odihnesc

Hurez Monastery, Tirgu Jiu

English	Pronunciation	Romanian
restaurant	rest-ow-RAHNT	restaurant
Where is a restaurant?	OON-day YEST-ay oon rest-ow-RAHNT?	Unde este un restaurant?
right		
To the right	la dree-AHP-ta	La dreapta
Right away!	REP-ed-ay!	Repede!
river	RUH-oo	râu
the river	RUH-ool	râul

English	Pronunciation	Romanian
road	DROOM	drum
the road	DROO-mool	drumul
Which is the road to ___?	KA-ray YEST-ay DROO-mool spray ___?	Care este drumul spre ___?
Romanian		
in Romanian	pay ro-mạ-NESH-tay	pe româneşte
room	KA-may-rạ	cameră

S

English	Pronunciation	Romanian
safety pins	AH-chay day see-goo-RAHN-tsạ	ace de siguranţă
salt	SA-ray	sare
Saturday	SUM-but-ạ	Sâmbătă
seat		
Have a seat	LWAHTS LOAK	Luaţi loc
seven	SHAHP-tay	şapte
seventeen	SHAHP-tay-spray-ZECH-ay	şaptesprezece
seventy	SHAHP-tay-ZECH	şaptezeci

74

English	Pronunciation	Romanian
shave		
I want to be shaved	ahsh vree-AH sǫ mǫ RAHD	Aş vrea să mă rad
shaving brush	pum-ǫ-TOOF day RAHSS	pămătuf de ras
sheets	chayr-CHA-foor	cerceafuri
shirt	kǫ-MA-shǫ	cămaşă
shoemaker	cheez-MAR	cizmar
shoes	GET-ay	ghete
shoelaces	shee-RET-oor day GET-ay	şireturi de ghete
shoe polish	KREM-ǫ day GET-ay	cremă de ghete
sick		
I am sick	SOONT boal-NAHV	Sunt bolnav
We are sick	soon-TEM boal-NAHV	Suntem bolnavi
sir	DOAM-noo-lay	domule
six	SHA-say	şase

75

English	Pronunciation	Romanian
sixteen	SHA-ee-spray-ZECH-ay	şaisprezece
sixty	SHA-ee-ZECH	şaizeci
sleep		
I want to sleep	ahsh vrea-AH sǫ DORM	Aş vrea să dorm
slowly		
Please speak slowly	vǫ ROAG vor-BEETS un-CHET	Vă rog vorbiţi încet
small	MEEK	mic
soap	sǫ-POON	săpun
shaving soap	sǫ-POON day RAHSS	săpun de ras
soup	SOO-pǫ	supă

The Olt River, Carpathian Mountains

English	Pronunciation	Romanian
English	*Pronunciation*	*Romanian*
speak		
Please speak slowly	vạ ROAG vor-BEETS un-CHET	Vă rog vorbiţi încet
spinach	spa-NAHK	spanac
spoon	LEEN-goo-rạ	lingură
spring	eez-VOR	izvor
start		
When does the movie start?	KUND un-CHEP-ay FEEL-mool?	Când începe filmul?
Stop!	STA-ee!	Stai!
store		
grocery store	buk-ạ-NEE-yay	băcănie
clothing store	ma-ga-ZEEN day HA-ee-nay	magazin de haine
Straight ahead	DREPT un-ah-EEN-tay	Drept înainte
street	STRA-dạ	stradă
the main street	STRA-da preen-chee-PA-lạ	strada principală

77

English	Pronunciation	Romanian
streetcar	trahm-VA_ee	tramvaiu
the street-car	trahm-VA-yool	tramvaiul
sugar	ZA-hur	zahăr
Sunday	doo-MEE-nay-kᴂ	Duminecă

T

English	Pronunciation	Romanian
tailor	kroy-TOR	croitor
take		
Take cover	ah-dᴂ-po-STEE-tsee-vᴂ	Adăpostiţi-vă
Take me there	koan-doo-CHETS-ee-mᴂ ah-KO-lo	Conduceţi-mă acolo
Take me to a doctor	koan-doo-CHETS-ee-mᴂ la oon DOAK-tor	Conduceţi-mă la un doctor
Take me to the hospital	doo-CHETS-ee-mᴂ la spee-TAHL	Duceţi-mă la spital
tea	CHA-ee	ceaiu
telegraph office	o-FEECH-oo tel-eg-RA-feek	oficiu telegrafic

English	Pronunciation	Romanian
the tele-graph office	o-FEECH-ool tel-eg-RA-feek	oficiul telegrafic
telephone	tel-ay-FOAN	telefon
the tele-phone	tel-ay-FO-nool	telefonul
ten	ZECH-ay	zece
Thank you	mool-tsoo-MESK	Mulţumesc
there	ah-KO-lo	acolo
Take me there	koan-doo-CHETS-ee-mₐ ah-KO-lo	Conduceţi-mă acolo
they	yay	ei
They are ___	YAY SOONT ___	Ei sunt ___
think		
I don't think so	NOO KRED	Nu cred
I think so	KRED	Cred
thirsty		
I am thirsty	MEE-yay SET-ay	Mi-e sete

English	Pronunciation	Romanian
thirteen	TRAY-spray-ZECH-ay	treisprezece
thirty	tray-ZECH	treizeci
this *or* that	AH-sta	asta
This is ___ *or* That is ___	AH-sta YEST-ay ___	Asta este ___
What is this?	CHAY YEST-ay AH-sta?	Ce este asta?
thousand	MEE-yay	mie
thread	AH-tsɑ	ață
three	TRAY	trei
Thursday	JOY	Joi
time		
What time is it?	KUT YEST-ay CHA-sool?	Cât este ceasul?
tired		
I am tired	SOONT o-bo-SEET	Sunt obosit
We are tired	soon-TEM o-bo-SEETS	Suntem obosiți

English	Pronunciation	Romanian
tobacco	too-TOON	tutun
today	AHZ$_y$	azi
toilet	la-TREE-nα	latrină
the toilet	la-TREE-na	latrina
Where is the toilet?	OON-day YEST-ay la-TREE-na?	Unde este latrina?
tomorrow	MWEE-nay	mâine
toothbrush	payr-YOO-tsα day DEENTS	periuţă de dinţi
toothpaste	PA-stα day DEENTS	pastă de dinţi
town	SAHT	sat
the town	SA-tool	satul
towel	pro-SOAP	prosop
train	TREN	tren
the train	TREN-ool	trenul
When does the train leave?	KUND plee-AH-kα TREN-ool?	Când pleacă trenul?
Tuesday	MARTS$_y$	Marţi

81

English	Pronunciation	Romanian
twelve	DOY-spray-ZECH-ay	doisprezece
twenty	DO-wą-ZECH	douăzeci
twenty-one	do-wą-ZECH shee OO-noo	douăzeci şi unu
twenty-two	do-wą-ZECH shee DOY	douăzeci şi doi
two	DOY	doi

U

English	Pronunciation	Romanian
undershirt	fla-NEL-ą	flanelă
undershorts	een-dee-spen-SA-beel	indispensabili
understand		
Do you understand me?	mun-tsay-LED-jets?	Mă'nţelegeţi?
I understand	un-tsay-LEG	Înţeleg
I don't understand	NOO un-tsay-LEG	Nu înţeleg

English	Pronunciation	Romanian
	V	
vegetables	lay-GOO-may	legume
	W	
Wait a minute!	ahsh-tep-TAHTS poo-TSEEN!	Aşteptaţi puţin!
want		
I want ___	ahsh vree-AH ___	Aş vrea ___
I want to ___	ahsh vree-AH sǫ ___	Aş vrea să ___
We want ___	ahm vree-AH ___	Am vrea ___
warm	KAHLD	cald
wash up		
I want to wash up	ahsh vree-AH sǫ mǫ SPUL	Aş vrea să mă spăl
Watch out!	ah-TENTS-yay!	Atenţie!
water	AH-pǫ	apă
boiled water	AH-pǫ F⌣YAR-ta	apă fiartă
drinking water	AH-pǫ day bǫ-OOT	apă de băut

WHICH IS WHICH?

SHOES

SPOON

LEEN-goo-ra
CHA-ee
SA-ray
GET-ay

SALT

TEA

(Answers in Word List)

English	Pronunciation	Romanian
hot water	AH-pǎ f‿yayr-BEEN-tay	apǎ fierbinte

we

We are ___	soon-TEM ___	Suntem ___
We don't have ___	noo ah-VEM ___	Nu avem ___
We have ___	ah-VEM ___	Avem ___
We want ___	ahm vree-AH ___	Am vrea ___
Wednesday	M‿YAY·R-koory	Miercuri

welcome

You're welcome	PEN-troo poo-TSEEN	Pentru puțin

well (for water) — fun-TUN-ǎ — fântănǎ

well

I am well, thanks	mool-tsoo-MESK, BEE-nay	Mulțumesc, bine

what

What is your name?	koom vǎ noo-MEETSy?	Cum vǎ numiți?

English	Pronunciation	Romanian
What's this?	CHAY YEST-ay AH-sta?	Ce este asta?
What time is it?	KUT yest-ay CHA-sool?	Cât este ceasul?
when	KUND	când
When does the movie start?	KUND un-CHEP-ay FEEL-mool?	Când începe filmul?
When does the train leave?	KUND plee-AH-kạ TREN-ool?	Când pleacă trenul?
where	OON-day	unde
Where are ___?	OON-day soont ___?	Unde sunt ___?
Where can I find ___?	OON-day poat gạ-SEE ___?	Unde pot găsi ___?
Where is ___?	OON-day YEST-ay ___?	Unde este ___?
which		
Which is the road to ___?	KA-ray YEST-ay DROO-mool spray ___?	Care este drumul spre ___?

English	Pronunciation	Romanian
Which way is north?	un CHAY dee-REKTS-yay yest-ay NOR-dool?	În ce direcţie este nordul?
wine	VEEN	vin
workman	loo-krạ-TOR	lucrător
wounded		
I am wounded	SOONT rạ-NEET	Sunt rănit
We are wounded	soon-TEM rạ-NEETS	Suntem răniţi

Patriarchate Church, Bucharest

Y

Yes	DA	Da
yesterday	YAYR_y	ieri
you		

Are you ___?	soon-TETS ___?	Sunteți ___?
Have you ___?	ah-VETS ___?	Aveți ___?

Arch of Triumph, Bucharest

Sibiu, Transylvania

Prefecture, Târgu Mureş, Transylvania